Francoise Gilot: The Muse Who Escaped Picasso

The Story of a Woman Who Found Her Own Voice

Theresa Brady

Table of Contents

<u>*Chapter one*</u>

Her Death News, Cause Of Death and Early Life (Biography)

Frances Gilot **(1921–2023)**.

Artist Françoise Gilot, who worked in Picasso's shadow, passed away at age 101.
She was long his lover and an accomplished painter (as well as memoirist) before she did something no other mistress of his had ever done: she walked out.

Françoise Gilot, a talented painter whose relationship with the much older Pablo Picasso overshadowed her work and who was the only one of his many mistresses to walk out on him, passed away on Tuesday at a hospital in Manhattan. She clocked in at 101.

Her daughter Aurelia Engel confirmed the death and noted that Ms. Gilot had been suffering from heart and lung issues lately.

Ms. Gilot quoted a surprised Picasso as saying, You imagine people will be interested in you? after she told him she was leaving him. They won't ever do it just for you. Even if you believe that others will like you, their interest in a person whose life has had such a profound impact on mine will only be mild.

Nevertheless, despite having a 40-year age difference, Ms. Gilot rebuilt her life after the relationship ended in 1953, unlike his two wives and other mistresses. She carried on painting, showing her work, and authoring books.

She got married to Jonas Salk, an American medical researcher who created the first reliable polio vaccine, in 1970 and spent some time in California. However, the public knew her best for her relationship with Picasso, particularly after her memoir, Life with Picasso, co-written with Carlton Lake, was released in 1964. It quickly became a best-seller on a global scale, which infuriated Picasso to the point where he cut off communication with Ms. Gilot and their two children, Claude and Paloma Picasso.

Ms. Gilot's candid and frequently sympathetic account of their relationship—she wrote the book to Pablo—served as a major source of inspiration for the 1996 Merchant-Ivory film Surviving Picasso, in which she was portrayed by Natascha McElhone and Anthony Hopkins played Picasso.

If Ms. Gilot's book did well, then her artwork has as well. Her paintings commanded rising prices well into her later years because they were featured in more than a dozen museums, including the Centre Pompidou in Paris, the Metropolitan Museum of Art, the Museum of Modern Art, and both in New York.

Paloma à la Guitare, a 1965 painting by the artist of a blue-toned portrait of her daughter, sold for $1.3 million at a Sotheby's online auction as recently as June 2021. That surpassed the $695,000 she received in 2014 for Étude bleue, a seated woman's portrait from 1953, at a Sotheby's auction, which was her previous record price. Additionally, as part of a retrospective of her work at Christie's in Hong Kong in November 2021, her abstract painting Living Forest from 1977 sold for $1.3 million.

After the 2021 auction, Lisa Stevenson, the head of curated sales at Sotheby's in London, said to ARTnews: It isn't widely known that Gilot's commitment to art was present long before her relationship with Pablo Picasso, and she was regrettably frequently left in his shadow.

Ms. Gilot favored letting others make assessments of her life and work. In a profile of her that appeared in the January 2022 issue of The New York Times, she stated, I am not going to make a big deal of being more than what I am — or less.

Born with money.

In a wealthy family, Marie Françoise Gilot was born on November 1. Emile Gilot, an agronomist and chemical manufacturer, and Madeleine Renoult-Gilot had just one child on June 26, 1921, in the Paris suburb of Neuilly-sur-Seine. Her 19th-century ancestors ran a couturier house of fashion that served Eugenia, Empress Napoleon III's wife, among other notable customers.

Her mother, who had studied art history, ceramics, and watercolor painting, encouraged Marie Françoise's interest in the arts from a young age. However, her father had other plans. Ms. Gilot remembered her father as an authoritarian who made her write with her right hand even though she was left-handed. He convinced his daughter to enroll at the University of Paris, where she earned her bachelor's degree in 1938 at the age of 17, anticipating a career in science or law for his daughter.

After graduating from Cambridge University with a degree in English literature, she continued her education by attending the Sorbonne and the British Institute in Paris. In 1939, as the war drew nearer France, her father sent her to Rennes, a city northwest of Paris, where she enrolled in law school. She never stopped working on her paintings.

She joined other students in a protest march against Germany at the Arc de Triomphe after the German occupation of Paris began in June 1940. Ms. Gilot was taken into custody, briefly held, and placed under watch after a confrontation with French and German authorities. She said of her family, We were not the kind of people who would become collaborators from day one.

At the University of Paris, she continued her legal studies; however, after passing her second-year exams in June 1941, she decided she was uninterested in the subject and would instead focus on the arts. She started taking private lessons from fugitive Hungarian Jewish painter Endre Rozsda and enrolled in courses at the Académie Julian, which boasted Matisse, Bonnard, Léger, and Duchamp among its former students. The decision, however, infuriated her father, and the two quarreled frequently until Ms. Gilot moved in with her grandmother.

Her first encounter with Picasso occurred by accident in May 1943, as Ms. Gilot detailed in Life With Picasso. In Le Catalan, a small eatery on the rue des Grands-Augustins close to Picasso's Left Bank studio, she was having dinner with her closest friend Geneviève Aliquot and an actor named Alain Cuny. At the time, Dora Maar, a Surrealist photographer, was Picasso's mistress. They were both seated at a different table.

Cuny was asked by Picasso to introduce him to the two girls. He invited them to visit his studio after learning that they were both painters. The next day, as well as a few more times before Geneviève left for her home in southern France, they did it together. Regardless of his growing attraction to her, Ms. Gilot persisted in visiting Picasso.

She spent a significant portion of that summer in Provence with Geneviève. Nevertheless, her friendship

with Picasso grew stronger during the winter of 1944. He was 62 and she was 22. She remembered later being completely exposed by his side. The impression that endures with me to this day is his extraordinary gentleness, she wrote.
He was very gentle, she said.

It would also be chaotic to be drawn into Picasso's world. Ms. Gilot recalled that German officers would visit Picasso's studio at least once a month in a 2007 interview for this obituary.

She said, They'd never be in uniform when they came, a group of five or six, and Pablo would ask me to follow them to make sure they didn't plant any documents they could 'find' later. That was something that always worried him.

Picasso entered politics by joining the French Communist Party after Paris was liberated in August 1944, when he was once more a well-known figure on a global scale.

Entering, leaving.

Dora Maar and his longtime mistress Marie-Thérèse Walter were still part of his life. Rightfully so, Maar started to worry that Ms. Gilot would take her place. A contentious chapter in Ms. Gilot's life began when she decided to move in with Picasso in May 1946.

Even though Ms. Gilot was depicted as a nymph to his centaur in Picasso's paintings and ceramics, which appear to reflect newfound happiness, he now appears to have felt as though he had defeated her and has reportedly started dating other women.

Paloma was born in April 1949, and Claude was born in May 1947. She continued to paint as well, choosing to imitate the School of Paris of the postwar period rather than Picasso. She held a successful exhibition in Paris in April 1952. Picasso, however, had already left without her and was on his way to the south of France. He also kept his new relationships a closely-guarded secret.

After all, in Sept. Ms. Gilot informed Picasso of her impending separation on October 20, 1953, while feeling unwell and unhappy.

According to her account in Life With Picasso, he retorted, No woman leaves a man like me. She said in her letter: I told him maybe that's how it appeared to him, but I was one woman who would and was about to. He said, I couldn't believe it, a man as rich and famous as he is.

Ms. Gilot had a brief relationship with the Greek philosopher Kostas Axelos, but she kept in touch with Picasso and even told him about her decision to wed her childhood friend, the French artist Luc Simon, in 1955. That union gave birth to her daughter Aurelia before divorcing in 1962, a year after Picasso wed Jacqueline Roque, his second wife.

Ms. Gilot and the artist's final disagreement centered on Life With Picasso. Her memoir was attacked by his friends and the French Communist Party, respectively. Picasso himself tried three times in vain to have the book banned from France. Then he said he wouldn't see Claude and Paloma ever again, and it appears he kept his promise up until his passing in 1973.

By that time, Ms. Gilot and Jonas Salk were wed, and she was commuting between her studio in southern France and her La Jolla neighborhood home in San Diego. She released a new book in 1975 titled Interface: The Painter and the Mask, which was a memoir of her career as an artist. She was appointed chairwoman of the University of Southern California's fine arts department the following year, a position she held until 1983.

She is survived by Ms. Engel, Claude Picasso, the head of the Picasso Administration, which looks after the artist's estate, Paloma Picasso, the fashion and jewelry designer best known for her perfumes, and four grandchildren.

After Salk passed away in 1995, Ms. Gilot moved to the Upper West Side of Manhattan, where she lived in a space that served as both a studio and an apartment. The space was described as an airy refuge with barrel-vaulted ceilings, towering bookcases, and an outsize window that bathes her canvases in a cool north light by Ruth La Ferla in the 2022 Times profile.

In addition to his prolific output, Gilot maintained a modest studio in Paris and held exhibitions in both Europe and the United States through 2021. She finished a book of sketches from 1974 to 1981 while visiting India, Senegal, and Venice. The sketches, many of which are in vivid color, were published in 2018.

Picasso's presence.

However, Picasso continued to be a commanding and, as a giant of 20th-century art, an overpowering presence even though he had been absent from her life for a long time and had already passed away.

Ms. Gilot wrote Matisse and Picasso: A Friendship in Art, a biography of the two artists' competitive friendship, in 1990 as she continued to think about him. It was a description of the friendship as it existed during the years she saw it. She and Picasso biographer John Richardson organized the popular exhibition Picasso and Françoise Gilot: Paris-Vallauris, 1943-1953 in 2012 at the Gagosian Gallery in Manhattan, which featured works they both produced during their time together.

Ken Johnson wrote in his review of the exhibition for The Times, Looking at the 30 paintings here, including naturalistic portraits of herself and her grandmother,

Cubist still lifes and abstractions, and pictures of herself and her children, you might think for a moment that you are looking at more Picassos.

When asked by Ms. La Ferla if she had ever felt competitive with Picasso or his friends, including Chagall, Braque, Matisse, and Giacometti, Ms. Gilot said, That never entered my mind. After all, I first picked up a paintbrush at age 3. You don't think in terms of me, me, me when you're a child. You are not capable of doing that.

But she admitted that those masters of the 20th century had an inevitable influence. She claimed that they helped me grow and that their interest helped her gain some self-confidence.

She said, I realized that if they are so big, then I am not so small.

Pablo Picasso came to Françoise Gilot's table with a bowl of cherries after she had just finished her meal at Le Catalan, a Left Bank restaurant in Paris. He had already undergone multiple self-reinventions and was 61 years old. She was 21 years old and just starting as a painter like the friend who was with her that night in May 1943.

After learning that the two beautiful young women were artists, Picasso exclaimed, That's the funniest thing I've heard all day. Girls like that can't be painters.

One of Ms. Gilot's paintings was a subtle jab at the city's Nazi occupiers, depicting a taxidermied hawk with the Eiffel Tower rising in the distance. This was the first time that her work had ever been displayed in an exhibition. She would carry on painting during the turbulent years that followed, becoming Picasso's mistress, model, and muse as well as the mother of two of his children and, according to his account, the only woman to ever leave him.

Ms. Gilot, a distinguished painter who passed away on June 6 at the age of 101 in a Manhattan hospital, had exhibitions of her work at the Metropolitan Museum of Art, Museum of Modern Art, and Centre Pompidou in Paris.

While battling those who sought to define her by the men in her life, such as Picasso, her friend Henri Matisse, and her second husband, American virologist Jonas Salk, who helped eradicate polio, she also published graceful, incisive memoirs and poetry collections.

She was undoubtedly influenced and motivated by those men, Ms. Gilot claimed. There was, however, no justification for viewing her as a supporting character as opposed to a central one. She told Mirabella magazine, Lions mate with lions. They do not reproduce with mice.

Françoise Gilot was born on November 1 in Neuilly-sur-Seine, a Paris suburb, the sole child of a wealthy agronomist. 26, 1921. Her mother, a housewife who also painted with watercolors and made ceramics, let her borrow paintbrushes when she was a young girl. She was pushed toward international law by her father, who yearned for a son and dressed Ms. Gilot in boy's clothing.

Like Picasso, her father expected brilliance and obedience, according to Ms. Gilot. To help her get over her fear of the water and heights, he made her swim and jump from heights. He made her practice writing with her right hand even though she was left-handed, making her ambidextrous. He advised her to adhere to a strict daily schedule that included eight hours of legal studies, eight more of painting, two hours of physical activity, and five hours of sleep to develop discipline.

Ms. Gilot earned a bachelor's degree in philosophy from the Sorbonne at the age of 17 in 1938. She was a law student in 1940 when the Germans invaded France. After that, she admitted to TV interviewer Charlie Rose, I started to wonder how long we would live. I will therefore carry out my wishes. '

When she started visiting Picasso's studio in 1943, following their initial encounter at the bistro, she had dropped out of law school at the Sorbonne, which started a years-long estrangement from her father. At the time, she was attending the Académie Julian art school. Picasso had already divorced his first wife, Russian dancer Olga Khokhlova, and started dating photographer Dora Maar by that time. Soon after, he left her for Ms. Gilot.

She described their relationship as a catastrophe I didn't want to avoid in her best-selling memoir Life With Picasso (1964). It was a passionate romance that was intellectually and artistically fulfilling but tarnished by incidents of physical and emotional abuse.

The couple cohabitate for almost ten years, spending most of their time at the La Galloise Riviera villa, where Picasso introduced Ms. Gilot to friends like existentialist philosophers Simone de Beauvoir and Jean-Paul Sartre, filmmaker, and artist Jean Cocteau, and painters Georges Braque and Matisse.

The latter acted like a visa on my passport to the world of art, Ms. Gilot said. Ms. Gilot recalled that Matisse was mesmerized by her graceful features and expressed his desire to create a portrait of her with olive green hair, light blue skin, and, of course, an angle between her eyebrows and nose. He compared her eyebrows to a pair of circumflex accents.

Picasso painted his mistress in 1946, using Matisse's suggested color scheme in a piece he titled La Femme-Fleur, apparently annoyed by the idea that someone else might paint her.

Later, he incorporated Ms. Gilot and their two children, Claude and Paloma, into sculptures, paintings, ceramics, and lithographs. But Ms. Gilot's work was more influenced by Matisse, whose vibrant, emotionally restrained style she valued over Picasso's expressionistic approach. Picasso biographer John Richardson stated that Picasso took from her rather more than she took from him when their works were on display together in 2012 at the Gagosian Gallery in Manhattan.

Stuart Preston of the New York Times wrote in his review of Ms. Gilot's 1965 solo exhibition at the Findlay Gallery in Manhattan showed that the artist was very much in her own right... Without any self-indulgent interest in sensuous or 'interesting' textures, she has a feeling for the quality of the paint itself and for the mysteriously effective relationship of color and shape that lends her paintings, large and small, a genuinely authoritative air.

Ms. Picasso eventually expressed his displeasure with Gilot's independence, saying that women were either goddesses or doormats. He put a lit cigarette to her cheek while they were arguing. He must have anticipated me to withdraw, she wrote, but she was adamant that she wouldn't let him have his way.

Another time, according to her, he allegedly pointed to a collection of trash in his studio and said, You don't count anymore for me than that dust there. The difference is that I am the kind of dust that prefers to be left alone and will leave on its own, she retorted.

Picasso allegedly tried to sabotage Ms. Gilot's artistic career after their 1953 separation by convincing some galleries not to display or sell her paintings, as a form of retaliation. He had less success trying to stop the release of her memoir, filing three lawsuits in a futile effort to stop it from happening.

The book, which Lake and Ms. Gilot co-wrote, included direct quotations from Picasso discussing his life and work, recited from Ms. Gilot's memory and accompanied, according to Lake, by letters and other memorabilia from their time together.

Supporters of Picasso denounced the book as libelous and vengeful. However, it has since evolved into a go-to resource for critics and academics, and one Times reviewer praised it for being a vivid portrait of a monstrously difficult man and a brilliant depiction of a great artist at work.

Its publication effectively ended Ms. Gilot's relationship with Picasso, who wed Jacqueline Roque in 1961 and reportedly forbade Claude and Paloma from entering his home. Ms. Gilot participated in the legal fight to win her children a share of his estate after he passed away in 1973.

By that time, she had already married and divorced Luc Simon, a French artist she had known since their student days; she frequently referred to it as her second marriage in an apparent nod to the intensity of her relationship with Picasso.

She wed Salk in 1970, who is arguably the most well-known doctor in the world thanks to his work on polio two decades prior. A friend of theirs put them in touch while he was managing a lab in San Diego. Salk had very little knowledge of science and almost none of painting. But Ms. Gilot claimed that when he invited her to tea and ordered pistachio and tangerine ice cream, it aroused her interest.

She agreed to marry him six months after they fell in love because of a shared interest in contemporary architecture. They remained together up until his passing in 1995. They split the year in half, with Ms. Gilot working from studios in New York and Paris as part of an arrangement that allowed them both to concentrate on their respective projects. She would occasionally paint while wearing a lab coat from the Salk Institute, according to People magazine.

When asked to compare her two well-known friends, Ms. Gilot remarked that Jonas Salk is the man's equal to the artist. Picasso the person was inferior to Picasso the artist. The bad luck that seemed to follow Picasso, including, she noted, the suicides of his mistress Marie-Thérèse Walter, his wife Roque, and his grandson Pablito, led her to eventually sell all the Picasso works she owned, including La Femme-Fleur.

When the Idyllwild arts school was a part of the University of Southern California, Gilot served as chair of the fine arts division. In addition, she co-authored the books Matisse and Picasso: A Friendship in Art (1990) and About Women (2015) with Lisa Alther. In 2009, she was made an officer in the French Legion of Honor.

Picasso's son, Claude Picasso, took on the role of estate administrator in the years following his father's passing. Paloma Picasso, her daughter, designed clothing and jewelry for Tiffany & Co. Aurelia Engel, an architect who took on the role of curator of her mother's archives, is another child that Ms. Gilot had from her marriage to Simon.

She painted until she was 90 years old, beginning at dawn while still in her pajamas and slippers despite losing vision in her left eye.

For his 2016 biography, The Woman Who Says No, she told journalist Malte Herwig that to truly live, one must take the risk of living on the edge. When you take a chance, you might also go through some bad things, but you'll mostly learn a lot and grow in life and understanding. Most importantly, you won't get bored. The worst scenario is boredom.

Engel said of her mother's departure, He never saw it coming. She was there because she loved him and firmly believed in the incredible passion for art that they both shared. She did so, nonetheless, as a liberated and incredibly young, but incredibly independent individual.

I was not a prisoner in the relationship, Gilot said to The Guardian newspaper in 2016.

The woman, who was 94 at the time, stated, I had been there of my own will, and I left of my own will. I once told him that before I left. Watch out, I warned, for I arrived when I pleased and will depart when I please. No one leaves a man like me, the man said. I replied, We'll see. '

Gilot published several books, the most well-known of which was Life with Picasso, co-authored with Carlton Lake in 1964. Its publication was attempted to be halted by a furious Picasso but in vain. Engel, 66, an architect by training who now oversees her mother's archives, claimed that he attacked her in court, and he lost three times. Nevertheless, she noted that after the third defeat, he called and congratulated her. He resisted it, but I believe that he was also proud to have been with a woman who had such bravery.

November baby born.

Gilot was born as the lone child on June 26, 1921, in leafy Neuilly-sur-Seine, a suburb of Paris. She was five years old when she decided she wanted to be a painter, according to Engel. She studied law because that was what her parents wanted, but her true passion remained art. In 1943, she held her very first exhibition of paintings.

When she and a friend visited a restaurant on the Left Bank that year, they happened to be surrounded by a group that included Picasso's former companion, Dora Maar. It was there that they accidentally met Picasso.

She writes in Life With Picasso, I felt that painting was already my whole life when I was 21. Gilot writes that when Picasso asked her and her friend what they did, the friend replied that they were painters, to which Picasso replied, That's the funniest thing I've heard all day. Painters cannot be girls who resemble that. The two were introduced after being invited to see Picasso in his studio.

The past ten years have seen Gilot's paintings achieve the recognition they truly deserved, according to Simon Shaw, vice chairman for global fine art at Sotheby's.

Shaw stated in an email that it was missing the point to view Françoise as Picasso's muse. When she first met Pablo, she was well along in her painting career. Françoise pursued a path that was fiercely her own; her art, like her persona, was full of color, vigor, and joy. Her work naturally interacted with his, but she also pursued a dialogue with him.

Engel observed that although her mother's relationship with Picasso was undoubtedly difficult, it also provided some freedom from her parents and the restrictions of bourgeois life, possibly allowing her to pursue her true dream of becoming a professional painter—a passion she shared above all else with Picasso.

They both held the view that creating art was the only worthwhile endeavor in life, she said. And even though life with him was not always easy, she was able to be true to herself. She was nevertheless able to be authentic.

And for Engel, her mother's most important legacy was not only her creativity but also her courage, which was demonstrated in her art, which was constantly evolving and never felt secure.

She was not fearless. But no matter what, she would always face her anxieties, leap into the unknown, and take chances, Engel remarked.

Gilot is seen twice.
Gilot was referred to by Picasso as the woman who says no, and their courtship was marked by a playful power struggle.

Chapter two

How a Master Became Picasso's Muse.

Both the artist's lover and the student was Françoise Gilot. She then yearned for more.

Françoise Gilot created the painting Adam Forcing Eve to Eat an Apple in 1946, not long after she fell in love with Pablo Picasso. At a table, two flat, angular figures are seated. As the man thrusts the fruit into her mouth, the woman calmly clasps her hands in front of her. The man is blocky, bald, and has one dark, piercing eye visible in his profile. In Gilot's interpretation of Genesis, temptation, knowledge, punishment, and exile are all things that come from man, even if the woman will ultimately bear the blame. Gilot resided with Picasso in the same year.
She was on the verge of disaster, a friend warned.

In her remarkable 1964 memoir, Life with Picasso, co-written with the art critic Carlton Lake and just recently reissued by New York Review Books Classics, Gilot recalls, I told her she was probably right, but I felt it was the kind of catastrophe I didn't want to avoid. The woman's eyes are open and bright in the painting.

At Le Catalan, a Left Bank eatery close to Picasso's residence and workplace on the Rue des

Grands-Augustins, Gilot, and Picasso first spoke in May 1943. She was 21 years old and had already come to believe that painting was her entire existence. The weeping woman in Picasso's paintings from the late 1930s was his lover Dora Maar. Picasso, who was forty years older, came over with a bowl of cherries to flirt. Later, he liked to claim that he had painted Gilot before she was born, back in his Blue Period. Gilot also creates the scene like a painting, contrasting the red of the cherries with the green of her turban and the intense bronze-green eyes of the scowling Dora Maar.

Green is the color of envy. Picasso's life included many other women besides Maar. He was still married to Olga Khokhlova, a former dancer for the Ballets Russes and a minor Russian aristocrat. Their marriage was a disaster—one glance at the saw-toothed grotesques he painted during their separation will reveal more about his feelings for her than you care to know—but French law prevented them from divorcing. Then there was Marie-Thérèse Walter, who was attractive and athletic, and whom he had wooed on the street when she was seventeen and he was 45. She, Maar, and their daughter Maya resided in an apartment close to his, while Maar did not; much to his amusement, the women hated one another. Maar, a well-known surrealist photographer, spent the entire day at home waiting for Picasso to call because he expected her to be completely available to him. Maar broke down as soon as he started dating Gilot. She told him the truth when he went to see her: As an artist, you may be extraordinary, but morally, you are worthless.

Picasso didn't like to hear this, but he didn't object. He claimed that women could be divided into two categories: goddesses and doormats. Gilot identified him as having a Bluebeard complex, which made him want to cut off the heads of all the women he had collected in his little private museum.

The heads were partially severed, though. To demonstrate that there was still some life left in them, that it hung by a thread, and that he held the other end of the thread, he preferred that life continue and that all of the women who had shared his life at one point or another continue to let out tiny peeps and cries of joy or pain and make a few gestures like disjointed dolls.

The Bluebeard tale is one of escape: just as he is about to behead yet another wife, her brothers swoop in and save her. So is Gilot's, but she saved herself. She stayed with Picasso for ten years, giving birth to two children, Claude (born in 1947) and Paloma (born in 1949), before divorcing him, making her the only one of his women to do so voluntarily, according to Picasso mythology. With that distinction, she gained morbid celebrity status, as if she were the only person to survive a plane crash. In front of her door, journalists camped. Even Pablo Picasso was in awe. In Vallauris, the Riviera town where they had resided, he had Gilot enter on horseback to begin a bullfight held in his honor as a fitting farewell to a worthy foe. The situation was worse off-camera. Gilot said she wanted to live with my generation and the problems of my time, and Picasso cursed her when she said that.

Even if you believe people like you, their admiration for someone whose life has had such a profound impact on mine will only be a form of curiosity. And all that will be left in your mouth after that is the taste of ashes. For you, the reality is over; it ends here. You're bound for the desert if you try to leave my reality, which has become yours since I discovered you when you were young and unformed and I burned everything around you.

Mostly, he was wrong. For starters, Gilot wed Jonas Salk in a happy union because he was confident enough in his abilities to adore her without regard for Picasso. Later on, she developed a renowned artistic career. Gilot, who has been painting for nearly as long as Picasso did at the age of 97, is currently experiencing a resurgence. I visited Sotheby's in October to watch a curator speak with her about a newly released Taschen edition of the imaginative travel sketchbooks she created while visiting Venice, India, and Senegal. Gilot was lucid, witty, and pitilessly dry in the French way while still looking stunning in a navy blue suit and a knotted silk scarf. Even though she has given many interviews about Picasso over the years, her interviewer had been told not to bring him up because it was her turn now.

However, it is also true that Picasso branded Gilot. As the muse who escaped, she took on the symbolic role of the rebel. In Life with Picasso, she signed her name next to his to show her appreciation for the way he had marked her reality.

Although her book ends with a rupture, it also begins with one. Gilot's wealthy agronomist father, like many other dejected haut-bourgeois fathers of the era (Simone de Beauvoir comes to mind), made up for having a daughter by rearing her as a son. She had a sense of calling, despite his decision that she would pursue a career in law. A sober young woman is depicted determinedly approaching her canvas in a self-portrait from the year she met Picasso.

Up until that point, my environment had formed a sort of cocoon around me that had protected me.
I thought that because I had been hearing life's noises so softly, I had lost all sense of reality. However, I was aware that an artist derives whatever quality of vision he brings to his work from his direct experience of life, so I knew I had to emerge from the cocoon.

Gilot told her father that she was leaving the legal profession to pursue art. He responded by beating her, taking away her income, and attempting to have her admitted to a mental institution. After moving in with her grandmother, she started painting and instructing riders at a stable. She proudly describes her habit of getting out of bed without even brushing her hair and going straight to her easel. In essence, this Neuilly-sur-Seine girl who had a good upbringing changed overnight to become a bohemian.

When Gilot first met Picasso, she was an independent woman who was thirsty for new experiences. The majority of the men she knew were enlisted in the Resistance, despite her attempts to get past that barrier called virginity for some time. The most well-known artist in the world was now showing her around his studio, introducing her to notable figures like Matisse and Gertrude Stein (both of whom were total sweethearts), talking with her about his work, and even encouraging her own.
He attended her debut exhibition and praised her for being very gifted in drawing.
Thrilled, she returned to her studio after hearing the comment.

Picasso, in a very different way, was also by himself.
The arrival of the Germans forced many intellectuals and artists from Paris.
However, he was obstinately but correctly convinced that he was invulnerable because of his fame.
He received special treatment even though he was considered the worst of the degenerates by the Nazis.
He boasted about his hot water supply and invited Gilot back for a bath when she first went to see him.

Her appeal to Picasso seems straightforward. She was attractive, young, and single.

Nevertheless, many girls were.
Her confidence, opinion, and lack of fear made her even more unusual.
She describes it as if she were a scrawny prizefighter getting ready to face the champion: I knew that there was something larger than life, something to match myself against.

She was referred to by Picasso as the woman who says no. He was funny, endearing, and expansive, and according to her, they had a complete understanding of one another. However, she soon realized what she might be getting into. When she arrived at the Rue des Grands-Augustins one evening, Picasso yelled that he would rather be at a brothel, according to her account. The irony is Gilot's go-to defense mechanism in unpleasant circumstances, and there were plenty of them. She calls him out coolly, saying that he is only trying to test her and doesn't even like whores. Yet she is cautious. She doesn't return for several months; instead, she only does so as a birthday present to myself. One of the few times that Gilot sounds as young as she was, this is both endearing and surprising.

Each of them constantly tries to throw the other off rhythm during their courtship, which was a playful struggle for dominance. He declares himself repulsed by her brazenness when she doesn't fight off his kisses. The victim and the executioner principal didn't interest me, she tells him when he tries to provoke her by making references to his sadomasochistic bedtime rituals.

Neither of those roles seemed to fit me very well, in my opinion. The book's most beautiful line is when the issue of sex is finally resolved during a nude modeling session. Afterward, he treats her with extraordinary gentleness, and that contrast, softness after so much sparring, results in the line: From then on, he became a person.

Few others had that impression of him. Gilot first visited Picasso's studio and discovered that it was the temple of a kind of Picasso religion, and everyone who was there appeared to be completely immersed in the religion—all but the one to whom it was addressed. He had been well-known for forty years when the war ended, and he became the mascot of the newly freed France. (He later became a member of the Communist Party, furthering his notoriety. Gilot recognized how Picasso, who benefited from this celebrity, was also made to feel alone. He took her on a pilgrimage to the Bateau-Lavoir, the run-down Montmartre building where he began his career alongside Max Jacob and Apollinaire—the last time he truly had a private life—early in their courtship. He bemoaned not having anyone to feed him while he fed the public (like a chicken). She claims that although she never told him, she could have.

Picasso's charming world has a carnival vibe, which can be lovely. As well as meeting Braque, who stands up to his former collaborator by inviting him over for a visit during which he displays his paintings but declines to provide any lunch, we see Matisse creating his cutouts (and flirting with his secretary). Picasso himself is the kind of magician who creates things seemingly out of thin air, including a novel lithography technique, unique glazes for his innovative pottery, and sculptures made from toy cars and scrap metal.

Gilot's personal Picasso is another example. The tyrannical moods are also childish—tantrums. He is superstitious, terrified of flying and getting his haircut, and needs to be coaxed, like a child, through insignificant decisions like how many tickets to buy for the bullfight. Picasso does not want Gilot to see a doctor when she is expecting Claude because he believes it will be bad luck, and she will then lose the baby. She is instead sent to Lacan for analysis.

Picasso's amanuensis, interpreter, money manager, model, and interlocutor is Gilot. She loads and unloads the car when they move houses. She stays up late with him, so she does too. She gets out of bed early in the morning to start the fires at home and in his studio because he very deftly pointed out that the space was only ever warm enough when I built the fires. More challenging is his treatment of the other women, whom he arranges before her like a maze: fragile, resentful Dora Maar; Marie-Thérèse, who writes him daily letters of love and cautions Gilot not to take my place. (Gilot reassures her that she needn't be concerned, saying, I only wanted to occupy the vacant one. Gilot does feel sympathy, even for Olga, who ambushes her and Picasso while they are on vacation and follows them in the street while yelling obscenities, though it would be a stretch to say that she expresses solidarity with her forebears. While doing so, Gilot examines them like a general going over lost battles, searching for weak points that she can plug with her own.

Of course, there is no way to verify whether or not everything that Gilot claims occurred did. (Lake claimed to have total recall, which is a claim more likely to arouse than allay doubts. She has the right of the memoirist, as I recall it, and Picasso's tyranny and brilliance are hardly in question. Gilot is the bigger mystery; it can be difficult to discern who she is behind her lacquered irony and reserve. However, she tells us, not at all for his reasons, she complies with Picasso's more bizarre demands and plans. Her disapproval is withering and sarcastic rather than ferocious; like other women of her generation who purposefully ignored their husbands' bad behavior, she is worried about maintaining her dignity. She is informed by her doctor (this time an obstetrician) that she is in danger and that labor must be induced right away when she is seven months pregnant with Paloma. Picasso, however, must attend a World Peace Conference in another part of Paris that day, so this is unfortunate for him. After much complaining, he decides that his driver will take him there and then return to pick up Gilot. This incident stands out even in a book filled with ghoulish caprice, but Gilot ignores it. When Picasso finally arrived at the hospital, she claims that he was wearing ripped, worn-out pants, which bothered her. Then she goes on for a while about how he can't afford new clothes. Gilot's anger, which was probably fueled by the man's egotism, was perhaps directed at his clothing in a typical case of displacement. But she had committed her entire life to him. He ought to at least don a respectable suit for her.

This type of anece was not well received by Picasso's admirers when Life with Picasso first came out; they branded Gilot a spiteful ingrate and rushed to exact revenge on the great artist. (He attempted to prevent the publication, and as a result, Claude and Paloma were never seen by him again. Picasso's biographer John Richardson wrote a scathing review of Françoise Gilot's wretched book, saying that she had the good fortune to be loved by the most inventive and creative artist of this century—perhaps of all time. (Subsequently, they grew close. Patrick O'Brian, the author of the Aubrey-Maturin books, met Picasso shortly after his breakup with Gilot. Gilot was portrayed in Gilot's biography as a selfish antagonist who had no concept of the stress that a creative person must endure.

These critics were quick to admit that Picasso hurt those around him, but they believed that brilliance ultimately excused wrongdoing. Art required sacrifice, especially for someone like Picasso, whose work was inspired by his own life. (Writing about Picasso's hatred of Olga, Richardson spoke of the rage, misogyny, and guilt that fueled his shamanic powers; you can almost smell the spilled blood. Currently, the widely held opinion is at the opposite pole. In her Netflix special Nanette last year, the Australian feminist comedian Hannah Gadsby

delivered an explosive skit about Picasso's treatment of women. She quoted some damning passages from Gilot's memoir and bemoaned Marie-Thérèse's situation in particular.
(Picasso sexually assaulted a minor)
That's it; I'm not interested. Gadsby couldn't care less about the art in comparison to these crushed lives.

Furthermore, lives were lost. At the age of 91, Picasso passed away in 1973. Marie-Thérèse Walter killed herself by hanging in 1977; Jacqueline Roque, Gilot's replacement and Picasso's second wife shot herself in the head eight years later. His son with Olga, Paulo, committed suicide by drinking himself to death in 1975, and Paulo's son, Pablito, killed himself by ingesting bleach after being denied access to his grandfather's funeral. This is a death toll straight out of a Greek tragedy.

Although some people may argue that women's lives were destroyed, at least they were immortalized as a result. According to Gilot, this was also the sentiment of his first love, Fernande Olivier, as well as Marie-Thérèse Walter, Dora Maar, and. The goal of Gagosian's Picasso's Women exhibition, which was mounted this spring, was to free Picasso's partners from their victimhood and restore them to their rightful place as the artist's muses. Blonde Venus Marie-Thérèse . is described in the exhibition copy's polished pinup prose. Picasso's depictions of each woman, according to Jacqueline Roque, the devoted, romantic beauty (Not how she presents herself to the world, but how she feels inside, capture not how she feels on the inside. Le Rêve (1932), a beautiful, serene portrait of Marie-Thérèse that Steve Wynn tore into a dozen years ago, was displayed on the show; if you look closely, you can see that half of her sleeping face resembles a phallus. She felt inside like this.

But it's difficult to argue that showing concern for these women's lives entails covering their painted faces with a cloth and leaving. It's possible that the more you know, the harder you'll search, and search, and search. You can gaze for all of eternity and still be curious about what you observe.

The story of a young woman who became enslaved to a charismatic master before ultimately escaping is told in Gilot's memoir, which is now recognized as a proto-feminist classic.
It is, however, a conventional love story as well.

The book itself contains incongruity. Near the end, she writes, I had felt that Pablo was a person to whom I could, and should, devote myself entirely, but from whom I should expect to receive nothing beyond what he had given the world through his art. On those conditions, I agreed to build my relationship with him. Gilot explains it simply: Love changed her terms. Where is the fierce, proud girl we met at Le Catalan. She desired more human warmth—to have a family—from Picasso. (He responded by engaging in another liaison. Unseemly pain starts to rise. She acknowledges crying constantly, calling it something feminine and—for me—most unusual.

The fact that Gilot had a brief affair with a potential suitor who was in her same age bracket and couldn't understand why she was obsessed with such a cruel old man was helpful in her quest to free herself. She also had her art. This sinister, delicious scene appears late in her book:

I once heard a small, timid knock at the door as I was working on a painting that had been giving me a lot of trouble.

Yes, I yelled, and I carried on with my work. Softly speaking from the other side of the door, I could hear Claude.

I adore you, mama.

Even though I wanted to leave, I was unable to do so because of my brushes. I continued working while saying, I love you too, my darling.

Several minutes elapsed.
Then he said, Mama, I like your painting, again, and I heard him.

I replied, Thank you, darling.
You're a saint.

He continued speaking after a further minute.
Mama, I appreciate what you do. It contains elements of fantasy, but it is not fantastic.

My hand was held still by that, but I remained silent. He must have noticed my hesitation. He now spoke more vociferously. It's superior to Papa's, he declared.

I went to the door and opened it for him.

Many women are familiar with the conflict between the mother and the artistic monster. Here, Gilot's ego strength is what stands out. What child—one who has been taught to flatter his mother—says that? It has a fantasy in it, but it's not fantastic.

Despite everything, she was concerned about what Picasso would accomplish without her. She was told to get over it; he would find another woman; who would light his morning fire. And he did: Jacqueline Roque, who presented herself as Gilot's submissive mirror image. When the new couple left Vallauris, Gilot returned to her old home and discovered that almost everything—her paintings, letters, and books—were gone. She was dropped as well by Picasso's dealer, Daniel-Henry Kahnweiler, who had started to represent her. However, she writes that she was appreciative of Picasso for completely severing their relationship: In doing so, he forced me to discover myself and, in doing so, to survive. She had the opportunity to do so ten years later. She made him the subject of her book.

Chapter three

Quotes by Françoise Gilot.

- Nobody is completely dependent on anyone else. You think he needs you or that leaving him will make him very unhappy, but if you do, he will have replaced you with another person in three months, and you'll realize that nobody is the worse off as a result of your absence. You must be allowed to act however you feel is right. If you can do anything else, nursing is not a viable profession. Your first and foremost thought should be about having to speak up on your own.

Tags: leaving Picasso, living for oneself.

- When I visited Picasso one day, we were watching the dust gyrating in the sunlight that was streaming in through one of the tall windows. Nobody truly has any significance to me, he told me. In my opinion, other people are similar to those tiny dust particles that float in the sunlight. They can be expelled with just a few strokes of the broom. I told him that I had often observed in his interactions with others that he regarded the rest of the world as nothing more than a few grains of dust. But I countered that, in reality, I was just a speck of dust with the ability to move on its own and didn't need a broom. I was capable of leaving alone.

Tags: Picasso, human existence, significance.

- He assured me that going forward, everything I did and everything he did would be of the utmost importance: every word I said, every gesture I made, and everything that transpired between us would change us constantly. Because of this, he continued, I wish I could stop time right now and keep everything exactly where it is because I feel like this very moment is the true beginning. We are equipped with definite but unquantifiable experience. The sand will start to drain as soon as the hourglass is turned, and once it starts, it will keep draining until all of it is gone. I wish I could have done that at the beginning. If it would make things take longer, we should use the fewest gestures, and fewest words, and even try to avoid seeing each other. Because we have an unknown amount of everything, we must exercise extreme caution to preserve its beauty. Happiness especially has a finite supply. Everything that must occur for a love to exist, including its duration and content, must be recorded somewhere. If you could reach the maximum intensity on day one, it would be over. Therefore, if there is something you truly desire and would like to see develop over a longer period, you must be extremely careful not to place even the slightest impediment in the way of an excessive demand that might prevent it from expanding to its fullest potential over the longest amount of time. You must avoid touching the butterfly's wings if you want to preserve its sheen. We shouldn't mistreat something that will improve both of our lives. Everything else in my life only makes me feel heavy and dims the light. This interaction with you seems to be an opening window. It needs to stay open, please.

Tags: time, relationships, time, love, Picasso.

- I wanted to investigate my solitude after realizing that Picasso lived in a self-contained world and that his solitude was therefore complete.

Labels: solitary.

- We shouldn't be averse to invention. In nature, we find everything that is in us. We are, after all, a part of nature. It's acceptable if it resembles nature. When man sought to create a tool as beneficial as the human foot, he created the wheel, which he used to carry both himself and his loads. It's hardly a criticism of the wheel that it bears no resemblance at all to the human foot.

Keywords: Picasso, inventiveness, creativity.

- You see, a painting for me is a dramatic event that causes reality to become fragmented. I am more concerned with that dramatic action than with anything else. In my opinion, the pure plastic act is only incidental. What matters is the dramatic tension created by that work of plastic art—the moment the cosmos explodes and meets its demise.

Picasso, creation, and painting are some related terms.

- I depict autobiographies written by some people. No matter how unfinished they are, the paintings serve as the pages of my journal and are therefore legitimate. The pages that the future prefers will be chosen. Making the decision is not up to me. The feeling that time is passing me by more quickly is one I frequently experience. I'm like a river that flows on, dragging with it any microbes that grow in it, dead calves that someone may have thrown into it, or trees that grow too close to its banks. All of that is in my possession as I move forward. Even if those efforts are not necessarily pushed to their logical conclusion, the dramatic transition from one effort to the next in the painting captures my attention. Since I was able to halt the passage of time there, I can say with certainty that in some of my paintings, the effort has been exerted to its fullest and most successful extent. Even though I have a limited amount of time, I have an increasing amount to say, much of which is related to the way my thoughts are moving. You see, I've come to the point where it interests me more to watch my thoughts move than the actual thought.

Tags: Picasso, autobiography, and painting.

- There is a certain difficulty in establishing relationships in just that way, and in that difficulty, there is an interest, and in that interest, there is a certain tension, and for me, that tension is a lot more important than the stable equilibrium of harmony, which doesn't interest me at all.

Therefore, what interests me is to set up what you might call the rapport de grand écart - the most unexpected relationship possible between the things I want to speak about. It is necessary to rip reality to shreds in every sense. Everyone is unique, which is something people frequently forget. In nature, nothing is ever created twice. It is for this reason that I place so much emphasis on finding the rapport de grande écart: a small head on a large body or a large head on a small body. To awaken the mind, I want to draw it in an unfamiliar direction. I want the viewer to learn something from me that he wouldn't have learned otherwise. I emphasize this because it shows how different, for instance, the left and right eyes are. They shouldn't be painted in such proximity by the painter. They just aren't that way. Therefore, my goal is to get things moving, to provoke this movement by contradictory tensions, and opposing forces, and in that tension or opposition, to find the moment that seems the most interesting to me.

Tags: reality-of-a-painting, Picasso.

- You have to admit that almost everyone dislikes most women who lead active lives.

Francoise.

- I quickly realized that Pablo required a constant victor and a vanquished and that this was the root of the issue. I don't believe anyone who is emotionally mature could be content with winning, including myself. Being vanquished also served no purpose because Pablo quickly lost interest after you were victorious. I couldn't afford to lose because I loved him too much. What should one do in such a situation?

Relationship dynamics are a tag.

- I gradually came to understand that Pablo had a kind of Bluebeard complex and wanted to cut off the heads of all the women he had gathered in his museum through his numerous stories and reminiscences about Olga, Marie-Thérèse, and Dora Maar, as well as their ongoing presence just offstage in our own life together.

He didn't, however, completely remove the heads.

To demonstrate that there was still some life left in them, that it hung by a thread, and that he held the other end of the thread, he preferred that life go on and that all of the women who had shared his life at one point or another continued to let out tiny peeps and cries of joy or pain and make a few gestures like disjointed dolls. They occasionally offered a comical, dramatic, or occasionally tragic angle on things, and that was all good feed for his mill.

Possessiveness, relationships, and so forth.

- And you, you're an angel—but an angel from a hot place, he said mockingly. That makes you one of my subjects since I'm the devil. I may brand you.

Tags: angel, art, devil, love, Picasso.

- Because of the passing of my grandmother, I felt a greater sense of personal isolation—as though we were all dying alone, incapable of being stopped or assisted.

Tags: individual-solitude.

- It's ludicrous to even talk about (Marquis) de Sade, let alone indulge in all that when people are being tortured and suffering for real, not for sexual games. I have no interest either in being a victim or in turning others into victims.

Tags: picasso-creator-and-destroyer.

- Don't imagine you could ever take my place. I replied, I had never wanted to; I only wanted to occupy the one that was empty.

You're attempting to swim upstream against the current. What is there about the natural flow of the river of life that has shocked you so strongly that you should want to swim against the current, even against time? You ought to know you're lost even before you begin. I don't understand you but I love you and I suppose you are obeying the law of your being.

Tags: love-life-time.

- As I was growing up, whenever anything frightened me to any degree, it fascinated me at the same time. I felt the need of going too far simply to prove to myself that I was capable of it.

Tags: capable, fascinate, frighten, prove.

- I paint the way some people write their autobiographies. The paintings, finished or not, are the pages of my journal, and as such they are valid. The future will choose the pages it prefers.

So how do you go about teaching them something new? By mixing what they know with what they don't know.

Then, when they see vaguely in their fog something they recognize, they think, 'Ah, I know that. ' And then it's just one more step to, 'Ah, I know the whole thing. ' And their mind thrusts forward into the unknown and they begin to recognize what they didn't know before and they increase their powers of understanding.

Tags: learning, Picasso, teaching.

- Pablo had told me, that first afternoon I visited him alone, in February 1944, that he felt our relationship would bring light into both our lives. My coming to him, he said, seemed like a window that was opening up and he wanted it to remain open. I did, too, as long as it let in the light. When it no longer did, I closed it, much against my desire. From that moment on, he burned all the bridges that connected me to the past I had shared with him. But in doing so he forced me to discover myself and thus to survive. I shall never cease being grateful to him for that.

Because even if you are against a movement, you're still part of it. After all, both sides of a movement—the pro and the con—are just different facets of it.

You can't get out of your period. Whether you take sides for or against it, you're always inside it.
- Pablo Picasso.

Every time I change wives I should burn the last one. That way I'd be rid of them. They wouldn't still be here to make my life difficult today.
-Pablo Picasso after Francoise left him.

Chapter four

PABLO PICASSO AND FRANÇOISE GILOT: THE WOMAN WHO SAYS NO (BIOGRAPHY, LEGACY, ACHIEVEMENTS AND WORKS OF PABLO PICASSO)

For ten years, painter Françoise Gilot has shared the life of one of the most consequential artists of the 20th century. Fiercely independent, she finally ended their relationship and terminated the hold.

Through their decade-long tumultuous affair which had a great influence on both artists, this film sheds light on her unjustly overshadowed work and revisits a flamboyant period in Picasso's career. Maybe that would bring back my youth, too. You kill the woman and you wipe out the past she represents.

Pablo Picasso, whose full name is Pablo Diego José Francisco de Paula Juan Nepomuceno Crispiniano Mara Remedios de la Santsima Trinidad Ruiz Picasso, was a Spanish expatriate painter, sculptor, printmaker, ceramicist, and stage designer who was born in Málaga, Spain, on October 25, 1881 and died in Mougins, France, on April 8, 1973. He is regarded as one of the greatest and most influential artists.

Born: October 25, 1881, in Málaga, Spain.
France (age 91), April 8, 1973.
The following are some notable works: Absinthe Glass, Blind Man's Meal, Crouching Woman, Dream and Lie of Franco, Family of Saltimbanques, Girl Before a Mirror, Guernica, Harlequin, Last Moments, Les Demoiselles d'Avignon, Old Jew and a Boy, Portrait of Ambroise Vollard,
Movement / Style: Der Blaue Reiter Neue Künstlervereinigung, Analytical Cubism, Surrealism , Synthetic Cubism.

The enormous body of Picasso's work is still extant, and the legend endures as a testament to the tenacity of the disquieting Spaniard with the somber...piercing eyes who superstitiously believed that work would keep him alive. Picasso dedicated nearly 80 of his 91 years to creating art, which had a significant impact on and paralleled the growth of modern art throughout the 20th century.

Life and work.
young years.

Pablo Picasso was the child of drawing professors José Ruiz Blasco and Maria Picasso López. When he started taking lessons from his father in A Corua, where the family had relocated in 1891, at the age of 10, his unusual talent for drawing started to emerge. From that point on, his capacity to experiment with what he had learned and to create new expressive tools quickly enabled him to outperform his father. His father in A Corua switched his own goals to those of his son, giving him models and encouragement for his first exhibition there at the age of 13.

In the fall of 1895, the family relocated to Barcelona, and Pablo enrolled at the local art academy (La Llotja), where his father had taken up his final position as a professor of drawing. The family hoped that their son would succeed as an academic painter, and in 1897 it appeared that his eventual fame in Spain was assured. That year, his painting Science and Charity, for which his father acted as the doctor's model, received an honorable mention at the Fine Arts Exhibition in Madrid.

For the young artist looking to gain notoriety and live up to family expectations, the capital city of Spain was the logical next stop. By protocol, Pablo Ruiz left for Madrid in the fall of 1897 and enrolled at the Royal Academy of San Fernando. However, he thought the instruction was stupid and began to spend more time observing the world around him, taking notes in cafés, on the streets, in brothels, and even at the Prado, where he first came across Spanish art. The Museum of Paintings is beautiful, he wrote. First-rate Velázquez; some magnificent heads by El Greco; Murillo does not always convince me in his paintings. At various points throughout his lengthy career, Picasso would become fascinated by the works of these and other artists. A portrait of the bullfighter Pepe Illo and the drawing for one of the Caprichos, Bien tirada está, which depicts a Celestina [procuress] inspecting a young Maja's stockings, are two examples of Goya's works that Picasso copied in the Prado in 1898. In his later work, the same characters—Pepe Illo in a 1957 series of engravings and Celestina in a 1968 suite of etchings and engravings known as Suite 347—recur.

After becoming ill in the spring of 1898, Picasso spent the majority of the rest of the year recuperating in the Catalan village of Horta de Ebro with his friend from Barcelona, Manuel Pallarès. He had gained weight, learned to live independently in the country, learned Catalan, and—most significantly—had decided to forgo his art-school education and reject his family's aspirations for his future when Picasso returned to Barcelona in early 1899. Even worse, he started to sign all of his works with the initials P, indicating a clear preference for his mother's last name. R. Picasso; by the end of 1901, he had completely abandoned the Ruiz.

Picasso moved around a group of Catalan writers and artists in Barcelona who were looking toward Paris. They were his friends from the café Els Quatre Gats (The Four Cats, modeled after the Chat Noir [Black Cat] in Paris), where Picasso held his first Barcelona exhibition in February 1900, and they were the subjects of more than 50 portraits (in mixed media) on display. Additionally, there was a gloomy, moody modernista painting called Last Moments (later painted over), which depicted a priest visiting a dying woman at her bedside.

That particular painting was chosen for the Spanish section of the Exposition Universelle in Paris that same year. Picasso set out with his studio partner Carles Casagemas (Portrait of Carles Casagemas [1899]) to conquer, if not all of Paris, then at least a portion of Montmartre because he was eager to see his work in situ and experience Paris firsthand.

Paris' discovery.

Picasso's main artistic revelation during that trip (October–December) was color. Not the dull hues of the Spanish palette, the black of Spanish women's shawls, or the ochres and browns of the Spanish landscape, but brilliant color—the color of Vincent van Gogh, new trends, and a city celebrating a world's fair. Picasso captured daily life in Paris in the work Lovers in the Street (1900) using charcoal, pastels, watercolors, and oils. He honored his fellow Catalan Ramon Casas as well as French artists Henri de Toulouse-Lautrec and Théophile Alexandre Steinlen in Moulin de la Galette (1900).

After only two months, Picasso and Casagemas—who had grown depressed over a failed love affair—returned to Spain. Picasso left for Madrid, where he worked as an art editor for a brand-new publication called Arte Joven, after attempting but failing to amuse his friend in Málaga. Following his return to Paris, Casagemas attempted to kill the woman he loved before turning the gun on himself and passing away. The effect on Picasso was profound: more than just losing his devoted friend and possibly feeling guilty for having abandoned him, he gained the emotional knowledge and the raw materials that would inspire the works of the so-called Blue Period's intense expressiveness. A few months later in 1901, Picasso created two death portraits of Casagemas along with two funeral scenes (Mourners and Evocation), and in 1903, Casagemas was depicted as the artist in the enigmatic painting La Vie.

Painter Pablo Picasso's Blue Period.

Picasso traveled back and forth between Barcelona and Paris, gathering inspiration from one location to the next, between 1901 and mid-1904, when blue was the most prominent color in his paintings. For instance, his depictions of Barcelona street people—blind or lonely beggars and castaways in 1902-03 (Crouching Woman [1902]; Blind Man's Meal [1903]; Old Jew and a Boy [1903]) reflect his visits to the Women's Prison of Saint-Lazare in Paris in 1901–1922, which gave him free models and compelling subject matter (The Soup [1902]). Picasso was also preoccupied with the issue of maternity at the time when he was looking for subjects that would best express traditional art-historical subjects in terms of the 20th century (women were permitted to keep nursing children with them at the prison).

The relocation to Paris and the Rose Period.

In the spring of 1904, Picasso finally chose to settle down in Paris, and his art displays a shift in attitude and, particularly, a reaction to various intellectual and artistic currents. Guillaume Apollinaire, a new and significant friend, began to discuss the traveling circus and saltimbanques. These aimless wandering actors (Girl Balancing on a Ball (1905) and The Actor (1905) took on the role of an evocation of the artist's place in contemporary society for both the poet and the painter. Picasso made that distinction specifically in Family of Saltimbanques (1905), where, according to their mutual friend, the author André Salmon, he plays the part of Harlequin and Apollinaire is the strongman.

When Picasso started dating Fernande Olivier at the end of 1904, his circumstances also changed. During the years preceding Cubism, her presence served as an inspiration for numerous pieces, particularly during their trip to Gosol in 1906 (Woman with Loaves).

Picasso found it difficult to work with color and tended to use more Spanish (i.e. a palette with only one color.
From late 1904 to early 1906, the so-called Rose Period, which was characterized by earthy, fleshy, and ceramic tones, took the place of the Blue Period (The Harem [1906]). In particular, in 1906 (Two Nudes; La Toilette), Picasso appears to have been experimenting with color to approach sculptural form. This progression is evident in his Portrait of Gertrude Stein (1906) and a Self-Portrait with Palette (1906), as well as the impact of his discovery of ancient Iberian sculpture.

The Avignon Demoiselles.

Picasso started work on the massive composition known as Les Demoiselles d'Avignon (1907) toward the end of the year 1906. His violent treatment of the female body and the mask-like painting of the faces (inspired by a study of African art) have made that work contentious. However, the work was firmly rooted in art-historical tradition: a resurgence of interest in El Greco contributed to the space's fragmentation and the gestures of the figures, and J. Paul Getty's The Bathers, as well as Paul Cézanne's Bathers, were both prominent influences on the composition as a whole.

The Demoiselles, on the other hand—later named to refer to Avignon Street in Barcelona, where sailors discovered popular brothels—were perceived as a shocking and direct assault: the women were not conventional images of beauty, but prostitutes who challenged the very tradition from which they were born. Picasso chose to roll up the canvas of the Demoiselles and keep it out of sight for several years despite already having his collectors (Americans Leo and Gertrude Stein and the Russian merchant Sergey Shchukin) and soon to be a dealer (Daniel-Henry Kahnweiler).

Picasso and his new friend Georges Braque adopted a technique in 1908 that included elements they discovered in Cézanne's work, whose shallow space and distinctive planar brushwork are especially evident in Picasso's work from 1909. The striations and mask-like heads that Picasso and Braque had been using since

1907 were replaced by a technique that included these elements. Picasso's first significant career subject was still life, which he first began to paint after Cézanne. The sculpture Head of a Woman (1909) and several paintings that are related to it, such as Woman with Pears (1909), are examples of Fernande's cubist heads.

The following few years (1909–12) saw Picasso and Braque collaborating closely; this was the only time Picasso had ever collaborated in this way with another painter. Together, they created what is now known as Analytical Cubism. Early Cubist paintings were frequently misinterpreted by critics and viewers as merely geometric art. However, the artists themselves thought they were portraying a novel reality that broke with Renaissance convention, particularly in the use of perspective and illusion. To convey more information than could be fit in a single constrained illusionistic view, they might have displayed several views of the same object on the same canvas, for instance.

By re-presenting the shape of objects and their location in space rather than imitating them through illusionistic means, according to Kahnweiler, Cubism stood for the opening up of closed form. Apollinaire compared the analytic process of fracturing objects and space, light, and shadow, and even color to the way a surgeon dissects a cadaver. Beginning in 1909, this kind of analysis became a defining feature of Picasso's work, particularly in the landscapes he painted while visiting Spain that summer (Factory at Horta de Ebro). The

Accordionist (1911), one of Picasso's paintings of seated people who were frequently playing musical instruments, was painted between 1911 and 1912. These were followed in 1910 by a series of hermetic portraits (Ambroise Vollard; Daniel-Henry Kahnweiler), and in these paintings, Picasso combined figures, objects, and space on a grid. Monochromatic ochres, browns, and grays were the only color options once more.

Although they implicitly accepted inconsistencies like different points of view, different axes, and different light sources in the same picture, neither Braque nor Picasso wished to enter the realm of complete abstraction in their Cubist works. Additionally, both artists had to reconsider what two-dimensional elements, like newspaper lettering, meant in light of the inclusion of abstract and representational elements on the same picture plane. A song title like Ma Jolie, for example, could allude to things that happened outside the canvas and tell the story of Picasso's new mistress, Eva (Marcelle Humbert). However, it could also be a reference to compositional aspects of the painting, such as the role of flat pictorial elements that interact with other flat planes or curvilinear motifs. The lettering also gave rise to the strong implication that Cubist images could be viewed coming forward from the picture plane rather than regressing into it (as in the traditional perspective). The cubists also altered the shape of the image—using an oval, for instance—in a way that highlighted the fact that the canvas is the true space in a cubist painting.

Collage.
Picasso and Braque advanced the Cubist idea of work as a self-contained constructed object by gluing real paper (papier collé) and other materials (collage) onto their canvases by 1912. The reintroduction of color occurred during the Synthetic phase (1912–1914), even though the actual materials frequently had an industrial reference (e.g. or wallpaper with prints). The main subjects for both artists were still lives and occasionally heads. Additionally, the multiple references found in Picasso's Synthetic compositions—for example, curves that refer to guitars and ears at the same time—introduce a playful element that is present in a lot of his work (Student with a Pipe [1913]) and imply that one thing changes into another. For instance, Absinthe Glass (1914; six variations) combines elements of painting, collage, and sculpture. It is made of cast bronze and features a real silver sugar strainer welded to the top. However, the piece is neither a sculpture nor a collage nor a painting because the object has three dimensions, unlike planes, which refer to two-dimensionality. Thus, the piece of art vacillates between reality and illusion.

Picasso's life had changed by 1915, and in a way, his art had also. The painting he had been working on during Eva's illness, titled Harlequin, which depicts a half-Harlequin, half-Pierrot artist in front of an easel holding an unfinished canvas against a dark background, bears witness to his grief. Eva passed away at the end of that year.

Parade.
Picasso's circle was split up by World War I; some members, such as Apollinaire and Braque, enlisted while the majority of Picasso's Spanish compatriots went back to their neutral country. Picasso remained in France, and starting in 1916, his friendship with the composer Erik Satie introduced him to a new avant-garde group that was active throughout the war. The young poet Jean Cocteau served as the self-designated leader of that group of artists who frequently visited the Café de la Rotonde. Parade, a piece about a circus sideshow that included images of the new century, such as skyscrapers and airplanes, was created as the result of his idea to stage a wartime theatrical event in collaboration with Serge Diaghilev's Ballets Russes. Following his visit to Picasso for the sets and costumes, Cocteau went to Satie for the music. Although Picasso detested traveling, he agreed to accompany Cocteau to Rome, where they met Diaghilev and Parade choreographer Léonide Massine. Work on the project began there in 1917. Among the dancers was where Picasso first met Olga Khokhlova, who would become his wife.

The first Parade performance took place at the Théâtre du Châtelet in Paris in May 1917, and it was widely regarded as an attempt to erode French cultural unity. Picasso disarmed the public with the contrast between his essentially realistic stage curtain and the startling Synthetic Cubist constructions worn by the characters, the sideshow managers in the ballet, while Satie appears to have been the main target of criticism (partly due to his inclusion of airplane propellers and typewriters in the score).

Compared to the Cubist pieces that came before or occasionally appeared alongside them, Picasso's paintings and drawings from the late teens frequently appear unexpectedly naturalistic (Passeig de Colom [1917]). After his trips to Italy and his return to Barcelona in 1917 (Parade was staged there in November), a new Mediterranean spirit became apparent in his work, particularly in the use of classical forms and drawing methods. By deliberately turning to look at J, that was confirmed.

Early Pierre-Auguste Renoir and Ingres, as seen, for instance, in Picasso's portrait drawings of Max Jacob and Ambroise Vollard (1915). Picasso's Cubist work was also influenced in terms of direction. The artist gave his Cubist paintings (Saint-Raphael still lifes (1919); two renditions of the Three Musicians (1921)) a classical expression by sharpening planes, forms, and color.

Pulcinella.

Born in 1921, Paulo was Picasso's lone child with Olga. Picasso continued his collaborations with the Ballets Russes as part of his new status as the socialites' darling (aided especially by his wife and Cocteau) and created designs for Manuel de Falla's The Three-Cornered Hat (1919), Igor Stravinsky's Pulcinella (1920), de Falla's Cuadro Flamenco (1921), and Satie's ballet Mercure

(1924), working with the Soirées de Paris company. Picasso's surrealist-inspired ballet designs were described by André Breton as tragic toys for adults.

Surrealism.

Picasso had close ties to Surrealism, the most significant literary and artistic movement between the two World Wars, even though he never officially joined the group. Picasso was adopted by the Surrealist movement, including André Breton, who served as the movement's chief propagandist. Picasso's art was given a new dimension by his interactions with his Surrealist friends, especially the writers. Since the Demoiselles, many of the ideas supported by the official circle have been present in Picasso's work. Breton specifically referred to the Strange Woman in a Chemise (1913) when he said that the juxtapositions and fractured contours of the human figure in Cubist artwork could be seen as the creation of monsters. Furthermore, the dreamlike imagery that the Surrealists favored appeared to coincide with the notion of reading one thing for another, which is implicit in Synthetic Cubism.

Picasso benefited from the Surrealist movement by being introduced to fresh themes, particularly erotic ones, and by having the disturbing elements in his work reinforced. The numerous variations on the theme of bathers with their overtly sexual and contorted forms (Dinard series [1929]) demonstrate the influence of Surrealism, and in other works (such as the Crucifixion drawings and paintings [1930–35]), the effect of distortion on the spectator's emotions can also be interpreted as serving one of Surrealism's psychological goals. Picasso frequently experimented with the concept of metamorphosis in the 1930s, as did many other Surrealist authors. For instance, Picasso's depiction of the minotaur—a mythological creature that is half bull and half human and is traditionally thought to represent the struggle between the human and the animal—becomes both an allusion to that idea and a sort of self-portrait.

Finally, poetry served as the best medium through which Picasso's unique brand of surrealism could be expressed. In the year from February 1935 to the spring of 1936, Picasso almost entirely gave up painting as he started writing poetry. In the years that followed, he wrote the surrealist play Le Désir attrapé par la queue (1941; Desire Caught by the Tail), as well as poetry collections that were published in Cahiers d'Art (1935) and La Gaceta de Arte (1936, Tenerife).

Sculpture.

Because Picasso kept a large portion of his sculpture in his collection, his reputation as a significant 20th-century sculptor only emerged after his passing. In Julio González's Paris studio, Picasso started utilizing iron and sheet metal starting in 1928. Then, in 1930, he bought the château Boisgeloup (northwest of Paris), where he had space for sculpture studios. In 1931, Picasso started working on large-scale plaster heads there, using his mistress Marie-Thérèse Walter as his inspiration. Up until the end of his life, Picasso continued to create sculptures in a variety of mediums, including constructions that included found objects.

The 1930s.

Olga and her bourgeois circle of society friends maintained a hectic pace of life in contrast to his private life with the undemanding Marie-Thérèse. When Picasso moved to Boisgeloup, he lived covertly with Marie-Thérèse (with whom he had a daughter, Maya, in 1935), and she served as the inspiration for many of his lyrical, occasionally erotic paintings, in which he combined intense color with flowing forms (Girl Before a Mirror [1932]).

Once a new lover captured his attention, Picasso never truly distanced himself from the women who had shared his life. This is clear from his artwork, where one woman frequently transforms into another. For instance, in a private sketchbook (number 99 [1929]), Picasso's portrait drawings reveal his double life as the images of his then-secret mistress turn into terrifying depictions of wailing Olgas. The French photographer Dora Maar and started dating in 1936. The change in his own life came at the same time as a time when he was personally preoccupied with the Spanish Civil War, which had started that year.

Guernica by Pablo Picasso.

Picasso visited his home country in 1934 but never went back, but he always had sympathies for Spain (the short-lived Republican government made him honorary director of the Prado), and in early 1937 he created a series of etchings and aquatints (Dream and Lie of Franco) to be sold in support of the Republican cause. The mural painting Guernica, which was commissioned by the Republican government for the Spanish pavilion at the 1937 World's Fair in Paris and named after the Basque town bombed by the Fascists, was undoubtedly his most significant contribution. Picasso was given a studio in Paris on the rue des Grands Augustins that was large enough to hold the enormous canvas (11 x 25 ft; 3 x 7 m; 77 m). His final piece of work, which took him just over three weeks to complete, was helped by Dora Maar. The imagery in Guernica—the wounded horse, the dead soldier, and the screaming mothers holding dead babies (representing the bullfight, the war, and female victims, respectively)—was used to denounce the pointless destruction of life, while the bull stood in for the possibility of defeating the unseen aggressor, Fascism.

Second World War and later.

Picasso's other works incorporate the expressive qualities of the forms and gestures in Guernica's largely monochromatic composition, particularly the intensely colored versions of Weeping Woman (1937), as well as related prints and drawings, portraits of Dora Maar and Nusch Éluard (wife of Picasso's friend, the French poet Paul Éluard), and still lifes (such as Still Life with Red Bull's Head [1938]). These pieces paved the way for the cramped interiors and skeleton-like drawings of the war years, which Picasso spent in France with Maar and

Jaime Sabartés, a friend from his time as a student in Barcelona. Following that, Sabartés shared Picasso's life as his secretary, biographer, and companion, and was frequently the target of never-ending jokes (Portrait of Jaime Sabartés, 1939; Retour de Bruxelles, sketchbook number 137, 1956).

Picasso resumed showing his artwork after Paris was freed, most notably at the Salon d'Automne in 1944 (also known as the Salon de la Libération), where his canvases from the previous five years were met with surprise. Demonstrations against Picasso's political views took place in the gallery itself as a result of that and the news that he had recently joined the Communist Party. At the same time, Picasso welcomed writers and artists into his studio, including many American GIs, Jean-Paul Sartre, Pierre Reverdy, Éluard, photographer Brassa, English artist Roland Penrose, American photographer Lee Miller, and many others.

Françoise Gilot, a young painter, first showed up at the studio in 1943. Within a few months, Picasso made her his mistress. With Gilot, with whom he would have two children—Claude in 1947 and Paloma in 1949—Picasso relocated to the Mediterranean in 1946. They first stayed close to Antibes, where Picasso painted at the Château Grimaldi for four months in 1946 while working on Joie de Vivre. Picasso's identification with the classical tradition and with his Mediterranean ancestry is vividly expressed in his works at the time, as well as the ceramics he decorated at the Vallauris studio beginning in 1947. They also rejoice over his newfound love for Gilot, who is frequently depicted as a nymph in works from that era in contrast to Picasso's fauns and centaurs.

Pablo Picasso is a ceramicist.

Because they appear at first glance to be a somewhat frivolous exercise in the decoration of everyday objects, Picasso's ceramics are typically separated from his main body of work and are treated as less important. Picasso's hands reshaped, painted, gouged out, scratched, or left fingerprints on plates, jugs, and vases that were made by artisans at the Madoura pottery in Vallauris, and, for the most part, rendered them useless. Picasso worked with a sense of liberation when he turned to craft, experimenting with the play between decoration and form (between two and three dimensions) as well as between specific and all-encompassing meanings.

During that time, Picasso's fame drew an increasing number of visitors, including writers and artists, some of whom (Hélène Parmelin, Édouard Pignon, Éluard, and especially Louis Aragon) pushed him to get more involved in politics. Although he gave willingly (his dove was used for the World Peace Congress poster in Wroclaw, Poland, in 1949), it was more out of a sincere and lifelong sympathy with any group of oppressed people rather than a commitment to the communists. Picasso's optimism of those times is reflected in the two panels, War and Peace, which he started painting in 1952 for the Temple of Peace affixed to an old chapel in Vallauris.

The Picasso urban legend.

In the decades leading up to his death, Picasso's work had, in a sense, moved beyond criticism, and an aura of myth had grown up around his name after World War II. Even though there weren't many detractors who could keep up with his most recent work, there weren't many who did. One exception was the British critic John Berger, who in his 1965 book The Success and Failure of Picasso questioned Picasso's financial motivations and conjectured about his exaggerated public image. Even though at the time his work appeared to be far from mainstream non figurative imagery, Picasso's massive output (especially in painting and drawing) kept his name in front of the public. He used figurative imagery, for instance, to weave a sort of narrative within each series' numerous variations in the series that typified the working methods of his later years.

Picasso spent several years living alone, dividing his time between Paris and his home in La Californie, close to Cannes (starting in 1955), after his wife Françoise Gilot and their two children left him in 1953. Jacqueline Roque, who worked in the Vallauris pottery shop at the time he first met her in 1953, not only became his constant companion from 1954 on (they were married in 1961), but she also served as his muse, serving as the main inspiration for nearly all of his later work. They are both interred in the Vauvenargues castle, which Picasso bought in 1958. However, they resided in the Mougins villa Notre-Dame-de-Vie from the time of their marriage until Picasso's passing.

Art history.

Picasso frequently used the history of art as a theme in his later works. In his numerous prints, drawings, and paintings from that period, references to artists like Albrecht Altdorfer, Édouard Manet, Rembrandt, Eugène Delacroix, and Gustave Courbet can be seen. He sometimes seemed obsessed with the need to create variations on the works of earlier artists. Picasso frequently created a full series of variations on a single piece, with the most well-known possibly being the series on Velázquez's Las Meninas, which consists of 58 distinct images. Picasso occasionally altered a particular piece of art because he connected personally to it. For instance, he was drawn to Delacroix's Femmes d'Alger because the figure on the right looked like Jacqueline. More often than not, he appeared moved by the challenge of resolving in his unique way the difficult pictorial and narrative issues the more experienced artists had first set for themselves. Picasso was in a way writing himself into the history of art by collaborating with so many of his predecessors.

In Picasso's later works, there is a renewed sense of play. In the 1956 film Le Mystère Picasso, directed by Henri-Georges Clouzot, the artist, the sole star, acts like a conjurer, pulling off feats of magic with his brush. He turned paper cutouts into monumental sculptures. Finally, driven by the same impulse, he returned to his earlier oeuvre, just as he had done with the paintings of earlier masters, altering them in numerous ways. He once more used the circus and his studio as the setting for his characters, often including himself as an elderly acrobat or king.

Legacy.

Almost no artist of the 20th century could escape the influence of Picasso because of the radical nature of his work during the Demoiselles period. Furthermore, Picasso continued to be an innovator into the last ten years of his life, unlike other masters like Henri Matisse or Georges Braque who tended to stick to predetermined stylistic parameters. That led to misinterpretation and criticism both during his lifetime and since, and it wasn't until the 1980s that his final paintings started to be appreciated for both their own sake and for their profound influence on the next generation of young painters. Picasso was able to keep the majority of his body of work in his collection because he could sell his creations starting in the 1920s for very high prices. He owned about 50,000 works in various media from every phase of his career at the time of his death, some of which were given to the French state and the remainder to his heirs. Their display and publication helped to confirm the highest assessments of Picasso's amazing creativity and execution over more than 80 years.

When Françoise Gilot first met Pablo Picasso in 1943, she was only 21 years old. The two happened to be seated at the same table in the same restaurant one evening in Paris. Picasso, his then-girlfriend Dora Maar, and their friends were there, and Gilot was there with her friends. Picasso approached Gilot's table after the meal was finished, offering a bowl of cherries and a request that he visit his studio on Rue des Grands-Augustins. Gilot observed that Picasso did not look like the handsome animal depicted in Man Ray's well-known photographs from the 1920s and 1930s because he had already achieved international fame as an artist. She was nevertheless entranced. He was 61.

Of course, this is a well-known tale that was first told in her 1964 memoir, Life With Picasso, co-written with American journalist Carlton Lake, and is now being republished by the New York Review of Books Classics. Gilot describes a ten-year romance with Picasso in it. She shared the same aspirations to establish herself as a serious painter. She eventually moved in with Picasso after being persuaded to leave her family. She immediately took on the roles of pupil, partner, and assistant before becoming the mother of their two children, Claude and Paloma. The progression of her career as a painter and mother is less the focus of the book than Picasso's. Gilot saw Picasso's experiments with ceramics, as well as his groundbreaking sculpture, lithography, and assemblages, while the artist was residing in Vallauris in the south of France. A visit to Henri Matisse's house served as the inspiration for his famous 1946 painting La Femme-Fleur, which also featured Gilot as its subject. Matisse teased Picasso, telling him that if he were to paint Gilot, he should color her hair green. Gilot's hair in La Femme-Fleur has the appearance of leaves, and her stem-like body sprouts abstract limbs and breasts.

Early in the 1950s, their bond started to deteriorate. I believe that I loved Pablo as much as anyone could love another person, but the thing he accused me of later was that I never trusted him. I came onstage with an unavoidably clear vision of three other actresses who had attempted to play the same role and had all fallen into the prompter's box; he may have been right, but it would have been difficult for me to feel otherwise, Gilot writes. She also mentions Picasso's other two longtime mistresses, Dora Maar and Marie-Thérèse Walter, as well as his first wife Olga Khokhlova. Gilot was the only woman to have ever left Picasso out of all of them.

Despite being a best seller, Gilot's book was derided by Picasso's inner circle, most notably by future biographer John Richardson, who published a scathing review of it in the New York Review of Books in 1965 with the dismissive title Trompe l'Oeil: In Life with Picasso the artist's complicated relationships with family, mistresses, friends, colleagues, and dealers, not to mention his private business arrangements and even his sexual habits, are un. Gilot did indeed include open quotes from Picasso about his contemporaries. I don't like the flying violinists, cocks, and asses, or all the folklore, but Marc Chagall's canvases are painted, not just thrown together. Less sensational than they might be now, sexual liaisons were reported. Picasso cut off his two children with Gilot after the book's release. Claude Picasso stated to Michael Kimmelman for this newspaper in 1996, We tried and tried and tried to see him. My dad was sequestered in his home. He didn't personally pick up the phone. Paloma and I, therefore, traveled separately, jointly, twice or more a year. You have to understand that his house was remote and that we didn't live in the South of France. A young person without a driver's license found getting there difficult.

However, the book reads surprisingly current decades later. Picasso is depicted as brilliant and autocratic, possessive of Gilot but also irresponsible with her wants and needs. There are only two types of women, according to Picasso, and they are goddesses and doormats. Although the book doesn't diminish his artistic ability, it does in its unique way present a man who could be remarkably cruel and self-absorbed toward those who were closest to him. A candid portrayal of his entitlement, immaturity, and ego must now compete with the myth of his genius. Gilot and Picasso had more in common than not, according to Richardson, who became friends with Gilot, just a year before Gilot passed away.

Chapter five

A Recorded Interview of Gilot and her daughter

97-year-old Gilot and her daughter Aurelia Engel participated in a recorded interview.

Gilot seems more interested in talking about her work than her life with Picasso, which is understandable. An edited and shortened version of our conversation is presented below.

Thessaly La Force: How was the book received when it was first published in 1964?

I can't remember, Françoise Gilot. It had been so long.

TLF: Considering it today, so many years later, do you have any opinions?

FG: No, I'm not living in the past; I'm living in the present. I'm not sure, maybe in the future. I don't care because I only think about the day at hand and consider what will happen tomorrow to be important. I don't care about things like this happening on such a day, etc.

TLF: Without a doubt.

FG: Additionally, painting is not something that — let's say, if you were studying mathematics, you might be interested in numbers; however when studying painting, you are not. In a painting, you are not at all interested in any kind of story; rather, you are interested in the relationship between colors or shapes.

TLF: Do you believe there is less of a sense of narrative in painting, or is it more about, as you say, color or form?

Painting is about painting, says FG.

TLF: However, I don't paint.

FG: I realize that, but it's crucial.
because a lot of people believe that you need to be telling a story. You occasionally can, but it's not required.

Do you paint each day? TLF: What about you?

FG: I don't know.
I might be drawing, or I might be gazing outside.

TLF: What do you do for fun?

FG: Nowadays, painting comes as naturally to me as breathing. Normally, I exhale. I keep breathing. Simple to do.
It doesn't come from some enigmatic realm.

It is something that occurs daily for me and for every painter. It is the capacity to communicate your emotions and to work with your hands. That is how things work.

TLF: You're right.

Like writing a poem or something similar, says FG.
The same applies.

Yes, TLF.

FG: It reads less like historical prose and more like a poem.

How long does it typically take you to complete a painting?

FG: For as long as a day, a month, or a year.

TLF: Depending on the?

FG: It entirely depends. It's different for each of them. I might finish it tonight or wait six months to do so.
Nothing changes.
As we like to say, that has nothing to do with fish prices.

TLF: How can you tell when a painting is complete?

FG: Any eye, including mine, can see it.

TLF: Since your memoir is being republished this month, I wanted to ask you about the rumor that you and biographer John Richardson became friends after he famously wrote a negative review of your book when it first came out.

FG: Ah, so he didn't know who I was. He never met me, but based on what he had heard, he made a judgment about me. Then, when he met me, we grew very close. What can I say, many people believed that they would please Picasso by opposing me.
They did it for that reason.
They gave up on that notion when they realized he had no response.

TL: Wow. Interesting. I cherished it. I believe it to be beautifully told and written.

FG: On top of everything, I'm not saying anything controversial. the exact opposite. Since I was the one who knew him best, they were confident that my book would be superior to the others. They had to attempt to strike it first.

TLF: I agree.

And they did, says FG.

TLF: The book is much more about Picasso than it is about you. You don't appear all that much in the book.

FG: I suppose I am the eye that is observing a spectacle. I'm thinking about what I'm seeing, not the eye when I say that.

TLF: From what I can tell, you decided to concentrate on Picasso and made that decision. However, I would have also liked to read more about your life.

FG: Although the title would be different, I could write a book similar to that. I have the writing skills to do all of that. I've been producing poetry. Other writings I did. But if I write about Picasso, it has to be about Picasso.

TLF: Were you concerned about how readers might respond as you were writing it?

FG: I don't ever have any fears.
That's not how I roll.
I wouldn't do it if I were afraid to. But I'm not scared. Who or what should I be afraid of?

TLF: I'm unsure. Some people experience fear.

FG: Fearful of the fear itself.

TL: I agree.

However, that is foolish. You can say whatever you want about me, but I'm not a moron.

Nobody, in my opinion, would say that, TLF. The conversations you had with Picasso about art and his contemporaries like Braque, Matisse, and Chagall were among the most amazing experiences you described.

FG: Well, we were residing together for at least ten years, though I'm not sure how many years in total. We got to know one another through our interactions as well as our conversations, etc. It has been a long-term relationship. It's the kind of thing that is extremely important.

TLF: What changes did your artwork undergo during that time?

FG: Well, like anyone, like any painter, the artist's work changes depending on the experiences they have.
It works out like that.
Living is what you do. We can see that it has some sun today. We can contemplate the sun or, on the other hand, the absence of rain, in which case, we can contemplate the sun.
I'm not sure.
Sometimes the topics I write about have nothing to do with a plan. Maybe I didn't plan it at all. It occurs on its own. Being impulsive is crucial, in my opinion.

Picasso comes across as a brilliant individual who is also incredibly egotistical, according to TLF. Do you believe that to be a —?

FG: The first negative response came from the group of people who surrounded Picasso. They had to criticize my book first because they believed it to be superior.

TLF: I agree.

FG: Of course, I was much more familiar with everything than they were. I was aware that I would have to fight for it because I would not be popular with everyone. Not everyone would find it appealing.

TLF: You're right.

FG: That is possible. It happens that people like you. People occasionally don't. You must, however, be true to who you are and what the truth is; you cannot shape who you are by the expectations of others, whether they be positive or negative. There are only these two things that matter. Because of the question of why I should say something that the general public already believes, I don't believe I have to be true to what they believe.

TLF: That's right, that's right.

FG: I won't say it just once, I'll say it a lot: They only think; they are ignorant.

TLF: Some might consider that to be very brave. Do you believe that Picasso-like behavior is required to be a genius or a great artist?

FG: He was, in fact, ten times more selfish than I thought.
He believed he was a hundred times better than everyone else. He was therefore a hundred times more egotistical.

TLF: Is it possible to be a good artist while also being selfless?

FG: No. First of all, the word selfish is incorrect. because a true artist ought to have a huge ego. It happens frequently.

TLF: OK.

FG: Because he needs to convey both his personality and how it interacts with the rest of the world. A creative person is unable to respond to inquiries about I don't know what. In his response, he discusses his inquiries into reality.

TLF: In your opinion, do women artists face greater challenges than men?

I don't see how sex would make a difference in that situation, FG. We can probably pay attention to different things than a man would, so why should it be different to be a woman or a man? By reflecting on it and considering what a workable solution to that issue might be, a woman would have been able to better understand the truth about specific things.

TLF: However, I'm curious as to whether men are permitted to be.

FG: Why should we be permitted to be anything? We are not permitted to be anything. The first point is that.

TLF: OK.

FG: We don't need permission because permission would entail following orders verbatim, which is hardly creative. No matter if they are male or female, painters and writers express their opinions on a variety of topics. They should stay at home if they are unable to do that.

TLF: The final chapter, which discusses your choice to leave Picasso, was another aspect of the book that I particularly enjoyed.

FG: You think I remember what I wrote in the last chapter, or even the first one? No, because I don't spend my time contemplating my past. I created it for myself. I make an effort to be as truthful as I can when I write. If I'm done, I'm done. Why do I need to look again?

I concur, TLF. However, he makes a statement to you as you are leaving that sounds like you owe him money. Life without him won't ever be as enjoyable. You seemed to have had a great life after him, do you want to say something for the record in response to that?

FG: No. I knew. Each of us only has one life. Your actions and life must reflect who you are, whether they are good or bad. What is what is.

TLF: According to André Gide's description of you in the book, despite having many regrets, you never have any regrets. Consider it to be true, do you?

Regret is something you have not done, so why should I feel regret? I had finished that by the time I left.
I left because of this.
I didn't just hang around for the sake of it.

TLF: Without a doubt.
That is why I adore the book.

FG: I believe it's crucial to live without regrets. Regrets are the result of not doing something. Well, having done this or that would have been preferable, and as a result, it had an effect. Real life has that as its goal, and you deal with it as best you can.

You would know because you are much older than I am, TLF.

FG: Being true to yourself is the most significant thing in life. If you have the time, you can be honest with other people.

Chapter six

Francoise Gilot Alleged Net Worth and Frequently asked questions about Her and Pablo Picasso

Francoise Gilot's net worth.

One of the wealthiest painters, as well as one of the most well-known, is Francoise Gilot. On November 26, 1921, in France, Francoise Gilot, a well-known painter, was born. Francoise Gilot's net worth is **$5 Million** as of June 1st, 2023.

Francoise Gilot frequently asked questions.

Gilot left Picasso for what reasons?
Françoise Gilot, a painter, once said of her 10-year marriage to Pablo Picasso, He called me 'the woman who says no' because when I had to say no, I did. We had two children, Paloma and Claude. She ultimately decided to leave him though because she didn't want to be consumed by the great artist.

Exactly who received Picasso's wealth?
The granddaughter of Pablo Picasso is Marina Picasso (born November 14, 1950). She received a portion of her grandfather's estate, a fifth of it, and has largely donated

the money to support charitable initiatives for underprivileged children. She has five children and splits her time between Cannes, France, and Geneva, Switzerland.

Picasso had many children who weren't his.
In addition to Picasso's widow Jacqueline, there was only one legitimate child, Paulo. Claude, Maya, and Paloma were the three illegitimate children.

When did Françoise Gilot part ways with Pablo Picasso?

1953.

After putting up with Picasso's rage for ten years, she became the only woman to leave him in 1953. Gilot and Luc Simon were married in 1955 after they first met as artists in 1954. Although they were a happy couple with a daughter named Aurelia, they eventually divorced in 1961 while still on friendly terms.

What did Picasso own at the time of his death?
Four children were born to The Master and three different women. As of the time of his death, it was also estimated that he had **$4,05,000,000** in cash and **$1,03,000,000** in gold. Another time, Picasso lacked a will.

When he passed away, how much money did Picasso have?

$100 to $250 million.

Upon his passing in 1973, an auditor estimated Picasso's net worth to be between $100 and $250 million. A portion of Picasso's estate was sought after by his wives, mistresses, and heirs.

Who was the lone woman to leave Pablo Picasso?

Francoise Gilot.

The Woman Who Says No is how Pablo Picasso referred to Françoise Gilot.
Gilot, the only woman to avoid the intense attention of Picasso during their ten-year relationship, was tiny, talented, and feisty in addition to being an accomplished artist in her own right.

What caused Pablo Picasso to pass away?

congestion of the lungs.
91-year-old Picasso passes away.

Early in the morning, a doctor from the sleepy village of Mougins, close to Cannes, called and said: It was already too late when I arrived. It was stated that lung congestion was the cause of death.

Was a girl adopted by Picasso?

Picasso and Fernande Olivier, his first true love and longtime mistress, decided to adopt a 13-year-old girl from a Paris orphanage at one point. Soon after, we learn that Picasso's emotions veered dangerously from the paternal.

Who holds ownership of Picasso's rights?

You must obtain the Picasso Administration's prior written consent—the organization that protects the artist's rights—to reproduce and/or depict works by Pablo Picasso. The Pablo Picasso Administration oversees, collects, distributes, and manages the rights associated with his creative output.

Which of Picasso's paintings is the most expensive?

Pablo Picasso, a well-known artist, sold a painting for a record-breaking $106,482,500 one lovely evening in New York. The painting titled Nude, Green Leaves, and Bust set a record for the highest price paid for a Picasso artwork in the year 2010 auction.

How did Pablo Picasso treat his family?

That, according to Picasso, was how he treated his grandchildren. According to her, Picasso's second wife, Jacqueline Roque, would keep them waiting for two to three hours if they accompanied their father when he went begging for money. They would occasionally watch hungrily as Picasso gobbled up a meal.

Who is Picasso's newest wife?

Discover Jacqueline Roque, a biography of the young woman who protected Pablo Picasso's privacy and served as his inspiration for the final 20 years of his life. Pablo Picasso and Jacqueline Roque were wed in 1961 and remained together until his passing in 1973. Jacqueline Roque was born in Paris, France, in 1927.

What became of Picasso's wealth?
After Olga died in 1961, and at the age of 80, Picasso married Jacqueline. It was up to the lawyers to divide up his collection of artwork, homes, and possessions after his death because he had not made a clear division during his lifetime.

How many Picassos have been stolen?
Pablo Picasso currently holds the title of an artist with the most stolen works of art in the world, with more than 1,000 of his pieces having been reported missing.

Who was the lady who witnessed Picasso sobbing?
Picasso's partner Dora Maar, a passionate, powerful, and knowledgeable woman, served as the inspiration for The Weeping Woman.
They have a complicated and frequently tumultuous relationship, and this is frequently seen in the painting.

Why is Picasso's artwork so expensive?
First, the price of Picasso's paintings can be attributed to the law of supply and demand.
The price is steadily rising as original Picasso masterpieces are becoming harder to find.

Second, Picasso's artwork is regarded as exceptional and has developed a strong brand worldwide.

Who was Picasso's life partner?

Picasso's greatest love was possibly Marie-Thérèse Walter.

She was kind, obedient, and the model for some of his most sensual paintings and sculptures. Walter was the ideal model and muse for Picasso's Surrealist era due to her physique.

Picasso was already well-known when he passed away.

Picasso achieved fame during his lifetime, unlike many other famous artists who practically starved to death. In addition to thousands of his paintings, he also owned five properties, a sizable savings account, gold, and bonds when he passed away at the age of 91.

Which Picasso painting caused the biggest stir?

Those Avignon Demoiselles.

Despite his creative genius, the well-known artist was hardly a good person. Up until I read Miles J.'s book Picasso and the Painting That Shocked the World, I had no idea. It is regrettable that Picasso's Les Demoiselles d'Avignon was so shocking.

What does the full name of Pablo Picasso mean?

The Full Name of Pablo Picasso Is 23 Words. Pablo Diego José Francisco de Paula Juan Nepomuceno Mara de los Remedios Cipriano de la Santsima Trinidad Martyr Patricio Clito Ruz y Picasso were Picasso's baptismal names. He was given names based on several saints and kin. His mother, Maria Picasso y Lopez, is the Picasso.

What was Picasso's most recent artwork?

Self Portrait in Death Situation.
Pablo Picasso, Self Portrait Facing Death, Painting, 1972. Pablo Picasso painted until three in the morning the day before he passed away at age 91.

On Sunday, April 8, 1973, hours before his passing. Less than a year before his death, he finished his last famous self-portrait, Self Portrait Facing Death.

She truly was a woman of valor.

Such depressing news.

May she rest in eternal peace.

Amen!!!

Printed in Great Britain
by Amazon

46129881R00056